I0172662

OVER IT!

GROWN WOMAN CHRONICLES

MICHELLE DAVIS

CONTENTS

Independently Published

Copyright © 2020 MICHELLE **DAVIS**

All rights reserved. No part of this publication may be reproduced, stored in or introduced into a retrieval system, or transmitted, in any form or by any means, electronic, mechanical, photocopying, recording or otherwise without the prior written consent of the copyright owner.

ISBN 978-1-954613-07-2

Book Cover Art Design: SelfPubBookCovers.com/ Grapiko

SILENCED

*S*ilenced with no voice
    Without hope
Clothed in low self-esteem and what the world thinks of me
I am sad
I am who you say I am and nothing more
I am who you want me to be so tell me more
Lost in a world trying to be someone I am not
Haunted by bad relationships, and immature adult experiences
Numb to the feeling of love
Numb to the feeling of care
Numb to my thoughts
Unbothered, unconcerned
Lost

BLACK GIRL SHINE

*B*lack girl shine bright
Your skin glistens without light

Don't let anyone ever tell you that you are not right because your skin is not white

Beautiful like the night sky, rich in hue

Every shade from maple, chocolate, mocha, caramel, the perfect cup of morning brew

Black girl shine bright

You are a descendent of survivors

Your face carries history of struggle, triumph, and freedom

Stand proud, walk tall for you are who others want to be

Black girl shine bright

You are an achiever

You break barriers, start trends, and break down walls

Keep believing in yourself, and always follow your dreams

Black girl shine bright

Your inner beauty is divine

You are mimicked by the entire world trying to capture your essence

No one can steal your glow or the way your features show, surrounded by the melanin skin God blessed you to be in

Black girl shine bright

There is a bigger picture

You are more than your hair

You are not just the color of your skin

You are more than the box the world tries to put you in

Black girl shine bright

Beautiful girl, spirit of love, mother of the world, daughter of Africa, and hope for our future

Grab your torch and go light the way, and don't let anyone or anything get in your way

I AM NOT ASHAMED

I am not ashamed of the person who holds my name

My appearance is not an inconvenience

My existence is not an accident

My culture is not a fad

My history is not folklore

Don't get confused by revisionist memories

My ambitions are not fairytales that will never come true

When I walk into a room

I feel the confidence I exude

My regal stance warrants a glance and a round of applause for all the broken-down walls

I am proud of my person

I will not go into hiding

If the world doesn't like it, I check the mirror

Head held high; I walk with pride

SHE IS ME

*A*ll I ever wanted to be was me

No one else, just me

For some reason that was not good enough for others

Fortunately, it has always been good enough for me

The woman in my dreams I adored for years, innately I always knew who she was

Each presentation of an imposter my soul rejected yet the world accepted…my soul cried

As my soul cried my spirit fought to keep me alive

Pressing, pushing, making it difficult to live under the guise

Impregnated for years, needing to give birth

As my spirit swelled my mind and body were compelled to change, grow, and adapt

The pain with each push was becoming raw, and uncomfortable

I could no longer hide the person growing inside

My spirit was ready with my soul along its side

I held on tight and prepared for the ride

After years of pain, pressure, and false starts

I grabbed hold and pushed even harder, I decided to fight

For my birthright

My talent

My existence in this life

The world tried to stop me

My fears kept me hidden, but my due date is here

As I stood in awe gazing at her

I was taken aback by her beauty, courage, and peace

An awakening birthed from a long hard journey

She is here

In every crease of my smile

She is me

In every bat of my eyes

I see her, I see me

On this day, the mirror spoke back

The woman I had always wanted to be

The woman I am destined to be

I am here, and I am all I have ever dreamed I would be

WOKE

*a*s my hips get wide from swallowing my pride

My lids hang low from no sleep at night

I realize I am not living my best life

I am making too many sacrifices

My life

My heart

My health

My wealth

My dreams

My sanity

Stressing over some other man's destiny

Exhausting my body and mind on someone else's empire with a ladder they refuse to let me climb

As the days go on, I am tired

Trying to hold on to this reality in which my light does not shine

My bulb is dull, with moments of flickering that eventually fade into darkness

Taking deep breathes I try to find a way to continue

I try to find a reason and purpose to allow my ambitions to become fantasies

So, I won't continue to dream, as there is no future in fantasies, no goals to set, no reason to fight

As I close my eyes at night my heart pounds with the urgency of life

My energy is electric, pulsing through my mind and body ready to take flight

My alarm goes off, and the humming of the energy in my veins stop

Time to cut the cord, oxygen depleted

Coma

Rest

Time to regain my "Om"

I am better than that

Smarter than this

The rhythm and the pattern goes on

In a place of despair and oppression every day

I am living with rage and aggression

Got to be strong, fuel my soul, sing my song, rise above, find my voice and realize...

I have a choice

I am done being sorry, done being stressed

I have a choice in how I live

Time to step into my appointing

Releasing my body from the strain of my mental flaws and bad habits

Allowing my soul and spirit to merge, collide

Breath and silence

Listening to the hum

Listening to the vibration; Verve

A LETTER TO DADDY

I don't know what it feels like to have my daddy holding
my hand

Catching me when I fall

Letting me know I'm his all in all

Teaching me how to ride a bike

Showing me how to fly a kite

Watching me go on my first date

Taking pictures on my prom night

Standing proud at graduation

Showing joy and elation

No walk down the aisle

Oh, and let's not forget all the birthday celebrations

All missed, no card, just blatant disregard

Thankfully I have a village behind me

More hands and hearts than I could ever hope for

Teaching me

Guiding me

Watching me

Caring for me

Giving me all the love, I need

Forming a circle of protection, and abundant security

Because of them toward you, Daddy, I do not feel any animosity

I realize life is hard

Everyone is trying to figure it out

Daddy, I see you clearly

Without titles, labels, or what the world wants to make you out to be

I see you as a little boy, a young man, a grown man; a person trying to find your way

I do not hold a grudge, I do not place blame on you for not being there for me

I just want you to find your way to be the man you were put on this earth to be

WHY DID IT TAKE SO LONG?

Why did it take so long?

For me to sing my own song

Come into my own

Understand the rhythm of my life

Why did it take so long?

To feel the notes on my tongue

Form the words with my lips

Know that I do exist

Why did it take so long?

For me to listen to the beat of my heart

Know that I am alive

Feel the energy bottled up inside

Why did it take so long?

MY OWN TERMS

I've been hurt and am healing each day

I feel lost, no longer kneeling to pray

I don't know which direction to go

I know what I have been taught and how I have been raised

It is hard to follow that direction when I see the downtrodden outcome of living by those standards

I want to live my life, my way, on my terms

My life is not a repeat, do over for the women and men before me

My life is mine to design

Mine to breathe

Mine to live

Enslaved to expectations, enslaved to memories

Restricted to certain places, specific locations, and topics of conversations

Confined to levels, boundaries, and history

There is more to me the world needs to see

More in me that I need to achieve

Held back by fear

Surrounded by ignorance

I am coming into my own

The more I understand who I am, what I stand for, the more resistance I face

Don't throw a bible verse at me, no holy water needed

I am standing by my position to be who I was put on this Earth to be

I am taking my time to define my life

If you can't accept it, please keep your distance

HAPPINESS

*L*ooking in the mirror at my reflection

For the first time in my life, I recognize the person staring back at me

I know her

I believe in her

I trust her

She makes me proud

No longer do I see her stripes, for they have been covered by her wings

Grown from her ability to overcome, forgive, and move on

The haunting of the past no longer exists

The condition of pity and grief, no longer persists

A wide bright smile opens the gate to bring forth words of love, encouragement, positivity, and freedom

Pouring out from a soul with vivid coloration

Projected from a spirit of maturation

A keen awareness of self and realization

I am worthy

I am love

I am blessed

I am at peace

I am who and what I say I am

Happiness is my choice

Love is my disposition

I am forever changed

I DREAM OF LOVE

My tears flow like a hurricane

The weight of the world is heavy

A thunderous storm rocking me to my core

Lightning strikes, I am hit multiple times

My heart is full of pain from the storms of the past

I never learned how to dance in the rain

I want to move forward but am being held back

I want to move forward but keep getting attacked

My past just won't let go, and I keep holding on

Repeating the same mistakes, blinded by fog, I can't see through the haze

Trying to reach the sun, the light is too bright for my gaze

TAKING BACK MY HEART

*S*pent so much time being the best I could be

    Woman, girlfriend, lover

Any and everything you could ever want or need

I lost myself in you

It was difficult when I had to start anew

Had to find myself

Remember how to love myself

Most importantly, forget about you

I felt so much anger when I thought about how I let you run rampant in my life

I had to forgive myself, move forward

I had to relinquish the strife

Another lover, man or romance was not what I needed

I gave you something priceless, something that didn't belong to you, and I am coming to get it back

You never asked for it, desired it, or understood its worth

Instead you took it, never looked at it, and tossed it to the side

Along with every other woman's heart you had accepted claiming love, it was all a lie

Under your bed, like Barbie doll heads, were thumps of beating hearts

Bleeding, crying, beating, some even falling apart

Gasping for breath from the pounding in my chest I made the decision I was worth more than what I had accepted

I am coming for you, let the battle ensue, you have something that belongs to me

I am wiping my tears, reading self-help books, and listening to every song of liberation I can find

I am out of my bed; thinking about my future, instead of what I thought in you was my everything

I am stronger than before

Get your ass up and come open the door

Don't make me break it down, I am only going to warn you one last time

I am here to take back my heart, take back what is mine

LOVE DEFERRED

Our love was like a burning flame

Hot, unable to tame

You were my joy and you were my pain

My friend, lover, just like kin

Folks used to say, "Girl, that man is your mate, go ahead girl and set the wedding date."

Lost upon wishes and dreams to fulfill

Our love everlasting has been deferred until...

CLOSURE

$\mathcal{N}$either of us knew we needed it

Our actions showed we were still deep in it

The random phone calls

The yearly pop-ups

The awkward conversations starting with, "Just checking on you"

The sleepless nights

The failed relationships

The lack of confidence in next steps

At one point I was with you, and you were with me

I think we both realized we were never meant to be

I was never yours to have and you were never mine to keep

Our interaction was exacted to bring us closer to our true loves we were destined to meet

Without you I would not be the woman I am

Without me you would not be the man you are

Our relationships in life are richer, stronger, and cemented in love because of our past

Your wife would not be yours if you and I had lasted

My husband would not be mine if I had not accepted that you and I were soulmates, but not life partners

Our struggle to let go was not due to love, but convenience, and uncertainty

Familiarity and recognition of another does not compare to the deep passion, and acceptance of another; flaws and all

Throughout our relationship we never understood the purpose of our meeting

We could never understand why we could never work

A decade later, through closure, we gave permission for our minds to move on and let our hearts take over

By closing one door, sealing it permanently; no lock, no key, we were able to move forward

No regrets, no animosity, you just were not the right man for me

ONLY FOR ONE NIGHT

I know this is wrong but it feels so right

    Right in this moment, if only for one night

What are we doing?

Do we really want to cross this line?

You've been trying to make a move on me

Do you think this is the right time?

We both know this is lust, not a fated romance

The way you are looking at me lets me know you are willing to take a chance

I am not asking to be your woman

You are not asking to be my man

I can't believe this is happening

This was not part of the plan

One of us needs to stop this

We are going too far

Do we go up, say goodnight, or are you waiting for an invite?

Do I take a risk as you lean in close, grabbing my face for a kiss?

As our lips meet, the rise of our body heat tell me we both want more

Our words are hushed and my face is flushed

I can see in your eyes an adrenaline rush

My inner lady is tingling

My hands are mingling

In the palm of my hand I can feel your growth

Your volcano is swelling, getting ready to erupt

What are we doing?

How did we get here?

My mind is saying this is way too much

Have we gone too far, and can't turn back?

Should we take this upstairs for a 2nd act?

There is a need in me, and I can feel the need in you

Please forgive me for my hesitation, I am not trying to tease you

How can something so wrong feel so right?

I am trying to hold back but I am losing the fight

I'll make a promise to you if you make a promise to me

To take each other up on this opportunity

Where this will go, I don't know and I don't care

Open up the car door I will race you up the stairs

The tension has been mounting, this is long overdue

Satisfy me and I will satisfy you

Just make me one promise before we turn off the lights

No matter what happens, we will still be friends after tonight

RUNNING BACK TO YOU

Something about the way you do

Keeps me running back to you

Something about the way you smile

Keeps me hoping we will reconcile

I know I shouldn't want it

It's not the right thing to do

But it's something about the way you do, that makes me want to work things out with you

Loving you was not my best decision, what the hell was I thinking?

I've got to get my head on straight

You got me thinking about drinking

When you flash me that smile you make me want to stay

When you kiss my lips, you make all the pain go away

I know it's over, and you know it too

But there's something about the way you do that makes me want to be with you

I can't stop thinking about the good times that we shared

Can't put my heart on the line

This would make the thousandth time

Got you out of my bed

Now it's time to get you out my head

I must not have been important enough for you because you keep doing what you do

I know I've said this before, but today I am walking out the door

There's nothing you can do because I'm done running back to you

THANK YOU

*T*hank you for being inconsiderate, insensitive, unloving, and unreliable

I am so thankful for your display of vulgarity, violence; mental, physical, and emotional abuse

I just can't seem to find the words or actions to thank you for showing your true colors and disrespecting me, using me, hurting me, and neglecting me

Now I know what a man is not

Now I know what love is not

Now I know the difference between a boy and a man

I thank you for not walking me to the door, not checking to make sure I made it home, not paying when we went out, not ever taking me out

I thank you for not catering to me as a queen, but demanding I treat you like a king

Playing childish semantic word games and silly hateful dating games

Thank you for showing me the consequences of lust; I will better recognize love, and be more open to trust

Thank you for showing me that speaking the word love without actions gives validity to the phrases 'talk is cheap' and 'actions speak louder than words'

I thank you, for you have made me wiser, stronger, more experienced, and able to recognize a good man when I meet one

IF SHE ONLY KNEW

*I*f she only knew who you were when I was with you

Would she tuck her tail and run or would she write me out a check to pay me for all the hard work I have done?

If she knew what I knew would she still want to be with you?

Would she get down on her knees and pray that you won't go back to your old ways?

Would she leave or would she acknowledge you have truly changed?

I have often wondered if she knew the real you, what would she do?

The scheming

The lying

The cheating

The mistreatment

The games

Would she blame it on your youth?

Or would she take credit for your upgrade?

I know I sound scorned, but it is interesting for me to see

The changes in you that occurred after me

I hope for her sake she understands her mate

I hope your changes are evidence that God can work miracles and people can learn from their mistakes

Woman to woman, for her sake I hope the changes in you are true

Luckily for you, she only sees what you want her to

FANTASY

You tell me what to wear and how to fix my hair

Every day getting dressed is an audition

I wonder will I ever get the part

From my painted toes to my shoes and clothes

You make sure you choose them all

From my finger nail color to my make-up

You treat me like a porcelain doll

You like the way I talk, but you want to fix my walk, in your mind all eyes are always on me

You're the fashion police, if I break a law, I get a lesson from you on how to be "pretty"

As I put on the 6-inch heels, and the outfit you bought, in your eyes I see a round of applause

As you look at what you think is your creation you smile in amazement, and tell me you knew I had it in me after all

Your words are truly disturbing, you are hurting my feelings, I am not your mannequin

There is a person inside who knows who she is and I love myself flaws and all

Tired of this game

This is not me

I am not what you want and you are not what I need

The woman in the magazine, she does not exist

Like you, she is living in a fantasy

LOVE IS NOT SUPPOSED TO HURT

*S*taring in the mirror I am at a loss for words

    Reeling, my mind is thinking love is not supposed to hurt

As the tears fall down my face I am confused by the image before me

Who is she?

Who are you?

How did I get here?

Why did I allow this to happen?

Why do I feel so scared?

I can't believe what just happened

His hands were around my throat

I was gasping for air, grasping for life

With no rescue in sight, I started praying to the Lord to give me the strength to fight

What has gotten into him?

On my back, on the floor, legs flailing and kicking

Does anyone hear me?

I need to try to scream

If I don't make it out of this, I won't live to fulfill my dreams

Dear Lord, please give me the strength

I got the message; I hear you loud and clear, this man is not for me

Now please, please get me safely out of here

As my body started to lose grip

I began to surrender, no fight left

As I saw my future slipping away

My Lord sent help, praise God they came

It took two men to get him off of me

What if they had not been there?

Thank goodness I knew how to pray

As I stood staring into the mirror, I winced from the pain of his hands around my throat

I asked myself for forgiveness

I had let myself down

I knew better, was raised better; could not believe how low I had sunk

Love is not supposed to degrade

Love is not supposed to harm

Love is not supposed to bruise

Love is not supposed to hit

Love is not supposed to kick

Love is not supposed to punch

Love is not supposed to hurt

LOVE DEFERRED AND LOST

I thought I knew what I wanted
    I thought I knew it all

Taking a break and moving on

Should have been the best thing for all involved

My return was supposed to be wanted…awaited

You were supposed to be standing there at the door waiting for me elated

Time has a way of changing things

For me, for the better; for you, for the worse

With time I became wiser

With time you became foolish

What was our enemy, time or youth?

During our adolescence I thought we were fated

Over time, I realized our past was overrated

In love with an idea

In love with being in love

What happened to the man I once knew?

Was it time that changed you or was it our youth I outgrew?

I am sad to disappoint our fans

Putting an end to all their plans

No wedding date to be set

No love to conquer all

We were both tested and after much reflection, a love deferred has now been lost

BLACK WIDOW

I am shocked and appalled at what I am being called

   I was minding my own business when you came into my world

You thought you had me figured out

You thought you knew what I was about

Sadly, mistaken you stepped unaware

Blind-sided by aesthetics and the warmth of my lair

Distracted by my hourglass figure and curly hair

You came in closer as your friends said beware

As you sought to claim ground you looked around

You were caught up, stuck, how did it get this far?

As I stared into your eyes you were haunted and surprised

At a loss for words you were unable to get away

You opened up your mouth in an effort to speak

Aware of your thirst, I began to spray

Seductively I spewed my venom

You drank it and asked for more

How twisted is love when both can't survive

Once the capturer, now the prey

FORGIVE ME

*Y*ou wanted to be my friend

  The way it all happened was so innocent

You were going through a hard time

When I met you, your heart was full of pain

Like two peas in a pod

We were attached at the hip

As time went on, our feelings grew strong

Our adolescence went away, our relationship started to change

Late night phone calls, lasting until the rise of the sun to a new day

Walking in the park under the night sky and the twinkling stars

We talked about everything we wanted to be and how our relationship
had gotten this far

You called me your Queen

Always kept me on a pedestal

You adored me in secret

Desiring my heart, you stayed closer than most

Waiting for your chance to solidify a romance, year after year, no matter my dating situation, you always stayed near

You saw me as a challenge, you were a man after my heart

I never saw it coming but your feelings for me ended up tearing us apart

A man that I trusted

My summer companion

We had a good thing going

Why did we have to take a chance on romance?

You were already getting the best of me

Why couldn't you see how important you were to me?

I never saw an end to our being friends, but that day came in an awful way

You professed your love for me

You put your foot down

No more hanging on the side

You wanted me for a lifetime

As I looked into your eyes

I saw a love so true

I saw my best friend, a companion, but no lover or husband

I knew if I did not reciprocate our relationship would not be the same

I knew you wanted an answer and would no longer play my games

Our friendship was special

I will remember it all my life

I am sorry I could not give you what you wanted

Sorry I left you disappointed

I feel like such a fake

Not living up to your image of me

I just hope as time passes you've been able to forgive me

SINGLE

*W*alking around the house, I feel so alone

Imprints on the wall where pictures of you and I once hung

You are no longer here but your smell is still in the air

I miss you

I want you

I know I shouldn't care

I am torn up, messed up; my house is a wreck

Can't let you break me

Being your woman doesn't make me

Got to pull myself out of this despair

Looking into this glass of wine reminds me of this one time

The one time you held my hand, acted like my man, and treated me nice and kind

Too bad I can only remember that one time…

I know I made the right decision getting you out of my life

The few great moments we had were just that, few and far between

I have made up my mind, and as I am drinking my 5th glass of wine, I am thinking about how precious life is and how with you I wasted so much time

So, for now I am going to listen to old love songs

Read romance novels

Take some time to love me and appreciate my current circumstance:

Single; not available

Celibate; not having relations

Focused; loving myself

Singly-minded; working on me

GIVING YOU MY HEART

A woman's love is
Pure

Deep

Spiritual

Comforting

Protective

To receive the fullness of this love is sacred

To be invited into the room, allowed to see the door to a woman's heart is blessed

Every conversation

Touch and realization

Kiss on the cheek

Hand in hand walk down the street

The door widens, chain intact

A sliver of light, shining in bright as the door creaks open revealing the darkness within

Torn between the thoughts of my mind, and the love in my heart

I keep my hand steady on the knob

I am uncertain of the brightness of the light

Darkness is all I have known

Is this light from the seeds I've sown?

How much longer can I hide?

I have so much love growing inside

This connection, chemistry, and affection

In your face, I see my reflection

Hand on knob, chain still intact

Can I do this?

Can I let my guard down?

If I open this door, am I prepared for the feelings and vulnerability?

Am I able to block out insecurity?

What about my mental health, and emotional stability?

I am thinking too much, need to get rid of this anxiety

Unlatching the chain, turning the knob

Receiving the light and all its uncertainty

I am giving you my heart

I UNDERSTAND

*Y*ou think I don't know but when I am around your feelings show

The electricity in the air, the ease of our bodies to share a touch, slight and light

I Understand

When I come around your heart swells with joy

I see it in your beautiful eyes, which shine bright with so much emotion and intensity they burn brighter than the sun above a dry desert

I Understand

I know you desire me

Not for my body but for my love

You desire to be engulfed in the aura which is me

You desire to know me like no other ever has

Your desire is so strong that your body and mind are no longer on the same frequency but battling causing an uncontrollable imbalance making you say and do things out of character

I Understand

True love is something you have never felt before

Embrace it, embrace me, for there is so much more to explore

THE MOMENT YOU HELD MY HAND

I remember the moment you first held my hand

I remember the feeling because it felt different from any other man

It felt safe, warm, and everlasting

I knew that day we would be Best Friends, Mr. and Mrs.

I could see wedding bells and feel your tender kisses

I knew we would be together and weather any storm

Cold winter nights, warm summer days

Spring time flowers transitioning as our love blossomed year after year

Arguments and disagreements leading to tears

Conversations and revelations bringing out fears

Love and realization drawing us near

Whenever we get lost and can't find our way

I always remember that moment on that day

The moment you held my hand I knew we would be together

Love you, love us, always and forever

THE DAY THE STARS ALIGNED

*I*t doesn't happen all the time
But for us on that day the stars aligned
Two souls, two hearts
All in a perfect line
The timing was impeccable
I couldn't believe it myself
All the prayers, all the tears and finally you were here
From the second, to the minute to the hours of the day
Amazing how nothing and no one got in our way
How it all happened leaves me breathless with no words to say
I think about how close we were to never meeting
The obstacles and set- backs, all purposeful in design
The bad relationships, relocations, and miscommunications

It felt like our God was taking his time while we sat waiting for love on the sideline

Little did I realize each moment was getting us ready for a lifetime

Our love is magical, everlasting, and forever

A love like ours couldn't be rushed

Every situation, failed relationship, and gut feeling brought us to this place

I am so blessed to have you

In you I see God's grace

I know we talk it about it all the time; I just want to let you know how glad I am for us the stars aligned

HONEY, LOVER, FRIEND

*H*oney, Lover, Friend
　　　My lifetime partner to the end
Your bright white smile
Your dark curly hair
Your smooth chocolate skin
Oooh, my Honey, Lover, Friend
My boo thang
My shugga wugga
My cuddle bunny
My sugar bear
My black knight
My Mr. Right
My Mr. Man
If only you could understand

My solid rock

My confidante

My family

I give you all of me

So, in case you didn't know

Or if my feelings didn't show

I hope my words have expressed

You are my Honey, Lover, and Friend

DESTINY

*O*ur two souls manifested in time

    Created, nurtured, blessed

You exude love

From every pore, orifice and vein you are dripping with the perspiration of love

Our two souls united in flight; symbols of hope, faith, and trust

We soar through the sky ignited in a ferocious flame, unable to contain

You exude love

You make me want to change my name, drop my game, and have your namesake

Please don't get it twisted, I am not crazy in love

I am trusting in love, and believing in God, and opening up my heart

I saw you before I met you

You came to me in my dreams

Your soul cried out and my soul reached out to receive

You pursued me with your prayers, romanced me in song, and made love to me with your essence

When I awoke from my dream my lips which you kissed were singing a song only recognizable to

Our two souls manifested in time

Created, nurtured, and blessed

You exude love

PALPITATIONS

*I*f you only knew the power that existed in the beat of your heart

That sound means so much to me

More than you could ever know

In the beat of your heart I hear life

In the beat of your heart I hear the song of love your body sings for me

In the beat of your heart I feel safety and security

As my hand touches your face

Your heart begins to race

The intensity of your pulse

The relief in your eyes

As you open them you are surprised

As I place my lips onto yours

Your beautiful face I adore

As I hover above your face, I feel your breath

As I lay on your chest, I feel the warmth of your embrace

My heartbeat syncs up to match your pace

I love watching you sleep

No need to wake, sweet dreams my love, go back to sleep

PASSION

*I*n the late of night, I long for you
      To smell you, taste you, inhale all of you
Nothing is better than being with you
When your fingers brush against my face
As you engulf me in your embrace
Nothing else matters, the world could stop
As your hand slides down my thigh
I lift my head and look up thinking, "Oh my!"
Anticipating your touch
I get excited from the rush
You are such a tease, but always eager to please
As I twist and turn, the tension in my body grows
I am fighting to keep quiet but the sensation is too much
I cry out in ecstasy, taking a moment to catch my breath

Your sweat against my body, your hands around my breasts

I can't take much more

The passion is too much

My body is giving in; I am no longer in control

The weight of your body is taking over; all I can do is grab hold

As the waves come crashing down, I think I am going to drown

Harder and harder, I can't stay on top

Harder and harder, I feel myself drop

My body can no longer keep pace

I turn over and fall onto my face

Exhausted, my body trembles, and vibrates softly

You stand over me at full attention

With a lick and a few slurps, you are now out of commission

I PRAYED FOR YOU

*P*eople say you are too good to be true

    They ask me how I know you are real

I tell them I know because I prayed for you

I prayed for your Strength

Courage

Determination

Wisdom

I prayed for your Sense of humor

Kindness

Humility

Quick wit

I prayed for your Honesty

Responsibility

Loyalty

Commitment

I prayed for your Work ethic

Good credit

Good looks

Stability

I prayed for your Respect

Love

Honor

Open Heart

I prayed for your Health

Mobility

Temperament

Physique

I prayed for you to have eyes only for me

A heart for God

To be the head of my household

To be a mate for me

So, when people say you are too good to be true

I tell them you are, and I thank God because he answered my prayers and gave me everything I asked for when he gave me you

WEDDING DAY

*T*ake my hand, come closer to me

      We are here today, just like we said, for the entire world to see

Our dream came true, you have me and I have you

No earthly man or circumstance can mess with our God's divine plan

For some, it is a mystery how we came to be

Not for me, I knew instantly, you had me at hello

A few bumps along the way, praise God we knew better to stay

Nothing is perfect but when two are destined,

Manifested in time, the universe conspired, and the stars aligned

You kept running back to me, I kept running back to you

Every time both of us extending our hands letting the other know that our offer still stands

My soul cried out, Lord what do you have in store

He gave me what I asked him for, and in you, so much more

As you looked into my eyes, I saw tears forming at the corners

Tears of joy and happiness on our 1st day of our new life

You've been in my dreams, I've been in your heart

No matter what the world brings, nothing will tear us apart

With a three-cord strand, before God, our family, and Man

I am excited to be on this journey with you

I am proud to say on this day, you are my love, my life partner, and husband

www.ingramcontent.com/pod-product-compliance
Lightning Source LLC
Chambersburg PA
CBHW060425050426
42449CB00009B/2147